PRINCEWILL LAGANG

Redefining America: Trump's 2025 Political Revolution

First published by Lagang Princewill 2025

First edition

This book was professionally typeset on Reedsy.
Find out more at reedsy.com

Contents

1

Introduction

Donald Trump's return to the political stage in 2025 marks a defining moment in American history. After his initial presidency and the turbulent years that followed, his re-emergence signals a renewed effort to reshape the country's governance, policies, and global standing. His influence remains strong among a significant portion of the American electorate, and his comeback represents more than just another campaign—it embodies a movement that challenges the status quo. As he positions himself for another shot at leadership, Trump's approach will test the resilience of American institutions and the extent of his enduring political appeal.

This book delves into the driving forces behind Trump's resurgence, examining the political, economic, and social conditions that have created fertile ground for his return. It explores the ideological divide in the country, where some view him as a champion of national revival while others see his leadership as a source of controversy and division. The landscape of American politics has shifted significantly since his first term, and understanding the factors that fuel his comeback is crucial to grasping the magnitude of this moment. His political revolution is not just about reclaiming power—it's about redefining what leadership, governance, and democracy mean in the United States.

A key focus of this book is the strategic foundation of Trump's agenda and how he plans to implement sweeping changes across various sectors. From economic policies aimed at revitalizing American industries to immigration reforms and foreign policy shifts, Trump's blueprint for the nation is bold and polarizing. This book examines his vision for reshaping government institutions, handling opposition from political adversaries, and maintaining the unwavering support of his base. As his movement gains momentum, the nation stands at a crossroads where the direction of American governance could be drastically altered.

Ultimately, this book seeks to uncover the broader implications of Trump's 2025 revolution. Will his return solidify a long-lasting shift in American politics, or will it spark a wave of resistance strong enough to challenge his vision? As the election looms, the country is bracing for a historic moment that will define the years ahead. By analyzing the promises, risks, and potential outcomes of his leadership, this book offers a comprehensive look at the political, economic, and societal transformation that may unfold.

2

The Return of Trump

Chapter 1:

Donald Trump's return to the political spotlight is not just a comeback—it is a movement fueled by both his unwavering ambition and the loyalty of his supporters. After leaving office in 2021, he remained a dominant figure in American politics, using his influence to shape the Republican Party and challenge his opponents. His rallies, media presence, and endorsements kept him in the public eye, ensuring that his political relevance never faded. As the 2024 election approached, the growing dissatisfaction with the Biden administration, economic instability, and global uncertainties provided Trump with the perfect opportunity to reclaim his position.

One of the driving forces behind Trump's return is the unwavering support of his base. Millions of Americans who embraced his "America First" ideology saw his presidency as a rejection of establishment politics and a bold step toward reclaiming national pride. Despite controversies, legal battles, and political resistance, Trump's followers remained steadfast, believing that he was the only leader capable of restoring American strength. His ability to connect with voters on a personal level, using direct and unfiltered rhetoric, reinforced his influence and ensured his continued dominance within the Republican Party.

Beyond personal ambition, Trump's decision to run again was shaped by the broader political landscape. The perception of government overreach, concerns about border security, and frustrations over inflation and foreign policy missteps gave him a powerful platform. Many conservatives viewed his leadership as a necessary counterbalance to progressive policies, believing that his return would bring back economic growth, law and order, and a renewed sense of patriotism. With these factors in play, Trump's campaign became more than just a political bid—it became a declaration of resistance against what his supporters saw as a failing system.

As Trump officially launched his 2024 campaign, the political world braced for an unprecedented battle. His presence in the race not only reshaped Republican politics but also forced Democrats and independent voters to re-evaluate the future direction of the country. His return was not just about winning an election; it was about cementing his legacy and proving that his movement was far from over. Whether his resurgence signaled a return to strength or a period of deeper division, one thing was certain—Trump's political revolution was only just beginning.

3

America at a Crossroads

Chapter 2:

As 2025 unfolds, America stands at a defining moment in its history.

The country is grappling with a range of crises—economic struggles, political polarization, and global instability—all of which have intensified the demand for strong leadership. Inflation, job losses, and rising national debt have put financial pressure on millions of Americans, making economic recovery a top priority. At the same time, ideological battles over issues such as immigration, healthcare, and education have created deep divisions within society. With trust in the government at an all-time low, many citizens are desperate for a leader who can offer both stability and change.

One of the most pressing issues facing America is the growing divide between political ideologies. The country is no longer simply split between Democrats and Republicans; it is now fractured into multiple factions, each with its own vision for the nation's future. Conservatives believe that progressive policies have weakened America's foundations, while liberals argue that Trump's movement threatens democracy. The rise of independent and alternative political voices has further complicated the landscape, making it clear that America is in the midst of a fundamental transformation.

On the global stage, America's challenges are just as severe. Geopolitical tensions with China and Russia, ongoing conflicts in the Middle East, and shifting alliances in Europe have placed the United States in a precarious position. Many Americans feel that the country has lost its influence and that foreign policy failures have weakened national security. Trump's supporters argue that his leadership is necessary to restore America's strength, while critics fear that his approach could lead to further isolation and conflict. The question remains: can Trump's vision provide the stability and dominance that America seeks, or will it push the nation further into uncertainty?

As the nation stands at this crossroads, the 2025 political revolution becomes more than just an election cycle—it becomes a test of America's identity and future. The choices made in this era will determine whether the country moves toward unity or deeper division, economic prosperity or instability, global leadership or retreat. Trump's return represents both a challenge and an opportunity, and America must decide whether his revolution will lead to renewal or disruption. The outcome will shape the nation for generations to come.

4

Trump's Political Ideology

Chapter 3:

Trump's political ideology has always been a combination of nationalism, populism, and economic conservatism. From his first campaign in 2016 to his renewed push for leadership in 2025, his core message has remained consistent: America must prioritize its own interests above all else. His "America First" philosophy emphasizes strong borders, economic independence, and a rejection of globalist policies that he believes have weakened the country. Unlike traditional Republican leaders, Trump's brand of conservatism is not bound by strict party ideology—it is driven by loyalty, results, and a promise to disrupt the establishment.

One of the pillars of Trump's ideology is his stance on immigration. He has long argued that unchecked migration threatens national security, job opportunities, and cultural identity. His push for stricter border controls, deportation policies, and legal reforms has resonated with voters who feel that the government has failed to protect American interests. While critics accuse him of promoting division and xenophobia, his supporters see his immigration policies as necessary steps to preserve national sovereignty and prevent economic strain. The debate over immigration remains one of the most contentious issues in American politics, with Trump at the center of the conversation.

Economic policy is another key aspect of Trump's ideology. He champions deregulation, tax cuts, and trade policies designed to protect American industries. His opposition to multilateral trade agreements and reliance on tariffs to negotiate better deals reflect his belief that past administrations allowed foreign powers to take advantage of the U.S. economy. While his economic strategies have sparked controversy, they have also fueled job growth and strengthened domestic production, making them a cornerstone of his appeal. As he returns in 2025, his economic agenda continues to focus on self-reliance and challenging corporate and globalist influences.

Trump's foreign policy stance further reinforces his nationalist approach. He advocates for a strong military, reduced foreign aid, and a re-evaluation of America's role in global organizations such as NATO and the United Nations. His supporters argue that his policies deter adversaries and prevent the U.S. from being entangled in costly foreign conflicts, while his opponents warn that his isolationist tendencies could weaken America's global influence. As the world faces new geopolitical threats, Trump's foreign policy decisions will play a crucial role in determining America's future position on the international stage.

By understanding the core principles of Trump's political ideology, readers gain insight into what drives his leadership and decision-making. His movement is built on the belief that America must reclaim its power, both domestically and globally, through decisive and often controversial policies.

As his revolution unfolds, the true impact of his ideology will be tested, revealing whether it leads to national renewal or further division.

5

The Economic Blueprint

Chapter 4:

Donald Trump's return to power in 2025 is anchored on the promise of economic revitalization. His vision for America's financial resurgence rests on a combination of tax cuts, deregulation, and protectionist trade policies. Trump believes that reducing corporate taxes and cutting bureaucratic red tape will encourage businesses to expand, create jobs, and stimulate economic growth. He argues that his approach will empower small businesses and bring back manufacturing jobs that were outsourced to other countries. However, while these policies may lead to short-term growth, critics warn of potential long-term effects, such as increased national debt and widened wealth inequality.

Trump's past economic policies provide insight into what his second-term agenda might look like. His first administration saw record stock market highs, historically low unemployment rates, and a boost in consumer confidence. However, the latter part of his presidency was marked by the economic downturn brought on by the COVID-19 pandemic, leading to soaring unemployment and an unprecedented federal spending spree. As he seeks to implement another economic revolution, questions remain about whether his policies can withstand future economic shocks and global uncertainties.

Another key aspect of Trump's economic blueprint is his emphasis on trade and self-reliance. His "America First" policy discourages dependence on foreign economies and pushes for renegotiated trade deals that prioritize American workers. Trump has been a vocal critic of China's economic influence, vowing to implement stricter tariffs and limit China's access to American markets. Supporters see this as a necessary step to protect national interests, while opponents fear that aggressive trade policies could disrupt international supply chains and lead to retaliatory measures from global partners.

Despite his confidence in these strategies, Trump will face challenges in implementing his economic agenda. The rising national debt, inflationary pressures, and shifting global markets present significant hurdles. Additionally, opposition from Congress and resistance from financial institutions could slow down or alter his plans. Whether his economic vision will lead to sustained prosperity or deepen existing economic divides remains a crucial question for his presidency. The success or failure of his economic revolution will play a defining role in shaping America's financial future.

6

Trump and the Global Order

Chapter 5:

Trump's approach to foreign policy in 2025 is expected to be a continuation of his "America First" doctrine, but with new challenges on the horizon. His presidency has always been characterized by skepticism toward international alliances and a strong preference for bilateral agreements over multinational partnerships. Trump believes that the United States has been burdened by unfair global arrangements, particularly in trade and defense spending, and has vowed to renegotiate America's role in international organizations. This stance has fueled tensions with traditional allies and led to uncertainty about America's leadership on the global stage.

One of the key areas of focus in Trump's foreign policy is trade. He has long argued that past trade agreements, particularly with China, have disadvantaged American workers. In his second term, he is likely to double down on tariffs, sanctions, and economic restrictions to counter China's influence. While this may strengthen American industries in the short term, critics worry about potential trade wars and economic retaliation that could harm global markets. Trump's confrontational approach to economic diplomacy may reshape international trade dynamics, forcing other nations to reassess their reliance on the U.S. economy.

Military engagement is another critical aspect of Trump's foreign policy strategy. He has consistently advocated for a strong military presence but has also been reluctant to engage in prolonged foreign conflicts. His past decisions, such as withdrawing troops from Afghanistan and reducing commitments to NATO, reflect his belief that America should not act as the world's policeman. However, with rising tensions in Eastern Europe, the Middle East, and the Indo-Pacific, Trump will face significant pressure to navigate these conflicts while maintaining his commitment to reducing foreign intervention.

Diplomacy under Trump is likely to remain unconventional. His personal style of negotiation, often marked by unpredictability and direct confrontation, has drawn both praise and criticism. Some argue that his unorthodox methods have yielded results, such as improved relations with North Korea and revised trade deals with Mexico and Canada. Others fear that his disregard for traditional diplomatic protocols could weaken America's alliances and embolden rival powers. As global tensions mount, Trump's approach to foreign affairs will play a crucial role in determining America's position in an increasingly unstable world.

7

The Culture War

Chapter 6:

Beyond economics and foreign policy, Trump's political movement is deeply intertwined with America's ongoing culture war. His presidency has amplified debates over issues such as free speech, identity politics, race, gender, and religion, shaping the nation's social landscape in profound ways. Trump's ability to rally his base around these cultural flashpoints has made him one of the most polarizing figures in modern American history. To his supporters, he is a champion of traditional values and a defender against progressive overreach. To his critics, he is a divisive force fueling societal discord.

One of the defining aspects of Trump's role in the culture war is his stance on free speech and political correctness. He has positioned himself as an opponent of what he calls "woke culture," arguing that political correctness suppresses open discourse and weakens American institutions. His rhetoric often targets media outlets, academia, and corporate America, accusing them of promoting leftist ideologies at the expense of conservative voices. This has resonated with many Americans who feel that mainstream institutions have marginalized their perspectives, further deepening ideological divisions.

Issues of race and gender have also been central to Trump's cultural battles. His opposition to critical race theory, diversity initiatives, and progressive gender policies has galvanized conservative voters who believe these movements threaten traditional American values. At the same time, his critics argue that his rhetoric and policies have emboldened extremist groups and fueled racial and gender-based tensions. The debate over these issues continues to shape public discourse, influencing everything from education policies to corporate hiring practices.

Religion plays another crucial role in Trump's cultural influence. He has garnered strong support from evangelical Christians, positioning himself as a defender of religious freedoms and traditional family values. His policies on abortion, LGBTQ+ rights, and religious expression have reinforced his appeal among conservative religious groups. However, these positions have also intensified opposition from progressive activists who see his administration as a threat to social progress. As Trump's revolution unfolds, the culture war remains a battleground where the future of American identity is being contested.

8

The Power of the Media

Chapter 7:

By 2025, the media landscape has evolved significantly, but its influence on politics remains as powerful as ever. Donald Trump has always had a complicated relationship with the mainstream media, often portraying it as biased and hostile toward his presidency. During his first term, he frequently clashed with major news outlets, branding them as "fake news" while simultaneously using media coverage to dominate the political conversation. In his second bid for power, Trump has refined his media strategy, leveraging alternative news sources, social media platforms, and direct messaging to control his narrative and communicate with his base.

One of Trump's greatest strengths has been his mastery of social media, even amid efforts to regulate or limit his online presence. Despite previous bans and restrictions, he has found new ways to engage directly with supporters, bypassing traditional media gatekeepers. Whether through alternative platforms or direct messaging tools, Trump's ability to shape public opinion without relying on mainstream news outlets remains a key asset. His supporters view this as a way to counter what they perceive as media bias, while critics argue that it enables misinformation and deepens societal divides.

Beyond social media, Trump's influence extends to alternative news networks and independent commentators who amplify his message. Over the years, a growing number of conservative media figures, podcasts, and digital news platforms have provided an alternative to traditional outlets, creating a parallel media ecosystem that reinforces his views. This media network allows Trump to maintain a constant presence in public discourse, rallying supporters and countering opposition narratives in real-time. As traditional media struggles with declining trust, Trump's media strategy gives him an edge in controlling the public perception of his leadership.

However, media scrutiny remains a formidable challenge. Investigative reporting, fact-checking, and opposition narratives from major outlets continue to shape public opinion, often painting Trump as a controversial figure. While his base remains loyal, independent voters and moderates may be influenced by negative press coverage, especially on key policy issues. The battle between Trump and the media is far from over, and its outcome will play a crucial role in shaping his presidency's legacy and impact.

9

Trump's Approach to Governance

Chapter 8:

Trump's return to power in 2025 raises questions about how he will govern differently from his first term. His leadership style has always been unconventional, relying on direct action, bold decision-making, and a willingness to challenge traditional political norms. Unlike past presidents who worked within the established system, Trump has often positioned himself as an outsider fighting against Washington's bureaucracy. This approach has earned him praise for breaking political stagnation but has also led to criticism for creating instability and unpredictability in governance.

One of the biggest challenges Trump faces in his second term is working with Congress. His first term was marked by frequent clashes with lawmakers, even those within his own party. While he pushed through key policies like tax cuts and deregulation, his ability to pass legislation was often hindered by partisan gridlock. Learning from these challenges, Trump may adopt a more strategic approach, forging stronger alliances within the Republican Party while continuing to challenge Democratic opposition. However, his willingness to work within the system remains uncertain, as he thrives on confrontation and political upheaval.

Trump's interactions with the judiciary will also be crucial in shaping his governance. His first term saw the appointment of numerous conservative judges, including three Supreme Court justices, who have had a lasting impact on legal decisions. In his second term, Trump is expected to continue reshaping the judicial landscape, reinforcing conservative interpretations of laws on issues such as immigration, voting rights, and executive power. While this aligns with his political philosophy, it also raises concerns about judicial independence and the long-term effects on American democracy.

Ultimately, Trump's governance in 2025 will be influenced by lessons learned from his first term. His experience navigating political opposition, media scrutiny, and public backlash may lead to a more calculated approach to leadership. However, his fundamental style—marked by direct confrontation, bold policy moves, and an unfiltered communication strategy—is unlikely to change. Whether this results in greater effectiveness or further division will depend on how he adapts to the evolving political landscape.

10

Trump and the American People

Chapter 9:

Trump's political movement is not just about policies and governance; it is deeply rooted in his connection with the American people. His ability to mobilize supporters through powerful rhetoric and direct engagement has made him a political force unlike any other. Unlike traditional politicians who rely on structured campaigns and media endorsements, Trump's appeal is largely personal—he presents himself as a fighter for the common American, unafraid to challenge the establishment. This authenticity, whether genuine or performative, continues to resonate with millions of voters.

His strongest base of support remains among working-class Americans, particularly those who feel left behind by globalization and economic shifts.

Many blue-collar workers see Trump as a champion who understands their struggles and prioritizes their interests over corporate elites and political insiders. Additionally, his appeal extends to rural voters, evangelical Christians, and conservative-leaning minorities who appreciate his stance on social issues. His ability to connect with these demographics is a significant factor in his sustained influence.

However, Trump faces challenges in expanding his support beyond his core base. His polarizing nature has alienated many moderate voters, suburban women, and younger demographics who view his leadership style as divisive. While some appreciate his directness and strong stance on issues, others see him as a destabilizing force. To secure broader support, Trump may need to soften certain aspects of his messaging or present a more unifying vision for America's future—something he has historically struggled with.

Grassroots movements play a crucial role in sustaining Trump's political momentum. From local rallies to online activism, his supporters are highly engaged and often take initiative in spreading his message. This grassroots energy not only fuels his campaigns but also ensures that his influence extends beyond electoral cycles. Whether Trump can translate this enthusiasm into lasting political success will depend on how effectively he bridges the gap between his loyal base and the broader electorate.

11

The Threat of Resistance

Chapter 10:

Despite Trump's strong influence over his political base, resistance to his leadership remains a formidable challenge. Opposition comes from multiple fronts, including members of his own Republican Party who are wary of his unconventional leadership style. Some establishment conservatives believe Trump's approach disrupts the party's long-term stability, creating a divide between traditional Republicans and his loyal followers. While many GOP leaders publicly support him, internal conflicts often emerge over issues like policy direction, governance, and electability. This tension within his party could weaken his ability to push forward his agenda.

Beyond party politics, Trump faces significant opposition from grassroots activists and protest movements. Throughout his political career, mass demonstrations have erupted in response to his policies on immigration, healthcare, social justice, and climate change. These protests are often led by progressive groups, civil rights organizations, and young activists who reject his vision for America. Social media and digital platforms amplify these movements, allowing resistance to organize quickly and challenge his administration's policies in real time. The question remains whether these efforts will translate into political change or simply reinforce the country's deep divisions.

The political establishment in Washington, including career politicians, bureaucrats, and lobbyists, also plays a key role in resisting Trump's influence. Many within the government seek to maintain traditional political norms and see Trump's disruptive approach as a threat to institutional stability. This opposition manifests in legal battles, congressional investigations, and policy roadblocks that make governing more difficult. Additionally, the intelligence community, the judiciary, and other power structures continue to serve as checks on executive power, ensuring that Trump's policies do not go unchallenged.

To overcome this resistance, Trump employs his signature strategy: direct engagement with his supporters, unfiltered communication, and relentless political pressure. He often uses rallies, social media, and conservative media platforms to paint himself as a victim of a corrupt system, rallying his base against perceived enemies. While this strategy has worked in the past, it also fuels political polarization and increases tensions across the country. Whether Trump can navigate these challenges effectively will determine the success of his political revolution.

12

The 2025 Election: A Turning Point

Chapter 11:

The 2025 election is shaping up to be one of the most consequential in American history. With deep political divisions across the country, the stakes are higher than ever. Trump's campaign focuses on presenting himself as the only leader capable of restoring American greatness, emphasizing his achievements and warning against the dangers of returning to traditional political leadership. His ability to frame the election as a fight between the people and the establishment is a key component of his strategy, rallying his supporters around a shared vision of strength and resilience.

Key battleground states will play a decisive role in determining the outcome. States like Pennsylvania, Michigan, Wisconsin, and Arizona, which have swung between parties in previous elections, will be closely watched. Trump's team is expected to concentrate efforts on voter turnout, especially among working-class Americans, conservative-leaning minorities, and rural communities. Meanwhile, his opponents will focus on mobilizing suburban voters, young people, and independents who may be disillusioned with Trump's leadership. The battle for these key demographics will shape the direction of the election.

One major concern is the possibility of a contested election. Given the political climate and Trump's history of challenging election results, a close or disputed outcome could lead to legal battles, recounts, and nationwide unrest. Election integrity, mail-in voting, and concerns over voter suppression will be at the forefront of national debates. If the results are not immediately clear, both sides could dig in, leading to uncertainty and prolonged political instability. The response of government institutions, law enforcement, and the judiciary will be critical in maintaining order.

The implications of the 2025 election go far beyond Trump himself. The outcome will determine the future of American democracy, setting the tone for how elections are conducted and contested in the years to come. If Trump secures another term, his vision for America will likely become more deeply entrenched, reshaping policies and institutions for the foreseeable future. If he is defeated, the country will face a new phase of political realignment, as leaders from both parties seek to redefine America's direction.

13

A New America?

Chapter 12:

As Trump's political revolution unfolds, the question remains: What kind of America will he leave behind? His leadership has fundamentally altered the nation's political landscape, challenging long-standing institutions and reshaping the role of the presidency. Supporters argue that his bold approach has strengthened America's economy, national security, and global standing. They see him as a leader who has broken through bureaucratic inefficiencies and given power back to the people. If his movement endures, America could see a lasting shift toward nationalist policies, economic deregulation, and a stronger executive branch.

However, critics argue that Trump's leadership has deepened divisions, weakened democratic norms, and eroded trust in institutions. The rise of political extremism, social unrest, and growing hostility between opposing ideologies has raised concerns about the country's long-term stability. If these tensions continue to escalate, the U.S. could face ongoing political turmoil, making it difficult to achieve unity and progress. The legacy of Trump's presidency will depend on whether future leaders can bridge these divisions or if his style of governance becomes the new norm.

The impact of Trump's presidency extends beyond America's borders. His approach to foreign policy, trade, and international alliances has redefined the country's role on the world stage. Some nations admire his focus on nationalism and strong leadership, while others see his policies as disruptive and unpredictable. Whether America remains a dominant global power or shifts toward isolationism will depend on how future administrations build upon or reject Trump's strategies. The world is watching closely to see if America's leadership remains strong or if internal divisions weaken its influence.

Ultimately, Trump's political revolution forces America to confront fundamental questions about its identity, values, and future direction. Whether his movement leads to long-term transformation or is merely a moment in history, the consequences of his leadership will be felt for generations. The America of tomorrow will be shaped by the decisions made today, and as the country moves forward, it must decide whether Trump's vision aligns with its long-term aspirations.

14

Conclusion

The political landscape of the United States is entering a transformative period, with Donald Trump at the center of a movement that seeks to redefine the country's future. His return has reignited fierce debates over governance, democracy, and national identity, challenging both the political establishment and the American people to confront the direction they want their nation to take. Whether viewed as a bold restoration of American values or a disruptive force that threatens democratic norms, Trump's leadership in 2025 will shape policies and ideologies for years to come. The effects of his revolution will not only influence domestic affairs but also extend across international relations, altering America's role on the world stage.

Throughout this book, we have examined Trump's vision, strategies, and the forces that support or oppose his return to power. His ability to mobilize a loyal base, counter political resistance, and push forward his agenda will determine the success or failure of his movement. While some believe his leadership is necessary to reclaim American strength and independence, others fear the consequences of his polarizing approach. The political divide in the nation has never been more pronounced, and Trump's presence in the 2025 landscape intensifies both the hopes and anxieties of the American public.

What remains uncertain is the long-term impact of Trump's revolution. Will his policies create lasting economic and political change, or will they deepen divisions and lead to instability? Will America emerge stronger and more unified, or will this era be remembered as a time of turbulence and unrest? These questions will only be answered in the years ahead, as the nation navigates the consequences of his leadership. One thing is certain: the debate over Trump's influence will not end with an election; it will continue to shape the ideological fabric of the country for generations.

As America moves forward, the lessons learned from this period will serve as a blueprint for future leaders and citizens alike. "Redefining America" has explored the complexities of Trump's 2025 political revolution, offering insights into both its promise and its perils. History will be the ultimate judge of his impact, but for now, the country stands at a pivotal crossroads, faced with decisions that will determine its identity, stability, and place in the world for years to come.

www.ingramcontent.com/pod-product-compliance
Ingram Content Group UK Ltd.
Pitfield, Milton Keynes, MK11 3LW, UK
UKHW022005140225
455059UK00011B/371

9 789319 906166